Robbing Hood

Written by
Jill Atkins

Illustrated by
Andy Hamilton

Long ago, Robin Hood was living with his band of men in a big camp, deep in a green forest.

It was near the town of Nottingham.

They all had green or brown outfits, so they were not seen in the trees.

Robin Hood was the best archer ever.

He was good at hitting the target!

In the town of Nottingham, there was a bad man. He was the top man too: the Sheriff.

He took cash from hard-up men and handed it to the rich.

One night, Robin met a man in town.

"That Sheriff took too much cash from me," the man said. "So now I have no cash at all. I am skint! What can I do?"

"I will help you get the cash back," said Robin. "I will send a letter into the forest. All my men will come to help."

Robin sprinted back to the forest and stuck his letter on to a tree.

That night, Robin's men agreed that they did not like the Sheriff's rotten deeds.

"Come on, men," said Robin. "Let us set a trap and pinch the cash."

They waited for a week.

Then, one morning, the Sheriff sent his men out with a cart. They went along the track into the forest.

"That cart is loaded with silver coins for the rich," Robin said to his men. "We must attack. We will get the cash and then hand it back to the hard-up men."

Robin's band of men hid and waited.

When the cart went under the trees, Robin said, "Now!"

His men landed on the cart.

They had a big fight, but soon Robin's men took the cart.

The Sheriff's men ran off.

Now Robin had all that cash!

Did Robin keep the cash for himself?

Yes, he did! Off he went, with the silver coins in big bags on his back.

"I am so rich I will camp in the forest no longer," he said to himself.

So what did he do?

He erected a strong fortress.

And from then on, he had all the things he needed!

What a wicked man!

No! Just kidding!!

Robin handed all the cash back to the hard-up men.

Robin was a **good** man!